The
WEST HIGHLAND WAY

PHOTOGRAPHY BY DAVID PATERSON & MIKE MCQUEEN
TEXT BY DAVID PATERSON

CANONGATE PRESS & PEAK PUBLISHING

A Co-Publication by

Canongate Press PLC, 14 Frederick Street, Edinburgh EH2 2HB

and

Peak Publishing Ltd, 88 Cavendish Road, London SW12 0DF

Text: © 1992 David Paterson

Photographs: © David Paterson and Mike McQueen

First Published in Great Britain in 1992 jointly by

Canongate Press PLC and Peak Publishing Ltd.

Designer : Jonathan Allen

ISBN : 0 86241 411 3

Typeset in 13pt on 16pt Garamond 3 by Barnes Vereker Allen
Printed in Singapore by Toppan Co. (S) Pte.

Loch Lomond, from Conic Hill

Ben Nevis and Fort William

CONTENTS

Buachaille Etive Mor and the River Etive

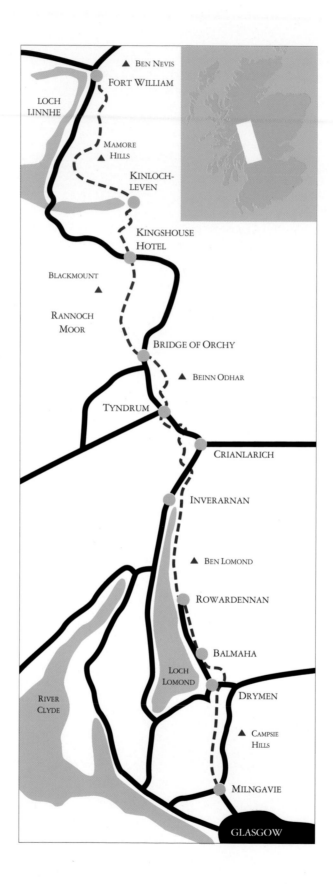

- BEN NEVIS
- FORT WILLIAM
- LOCH LINNHE
- MAMORE HILLS
- KINLOCH-LEVEN
- KINGSHOUSE HOTEL
- BLACKMOUNT
- RANNOCH MOOR
- BRIDGE OF ORCHY
- BEINN ODHAR
- TYNDRUM
- CRIANLARICH
- INVERARNAN
- BEN LOMOND
- ROWARDENNAN
- BALMAHA
- LOCH LOMOND
- RIVER CLYDE
- DRYMEN
- CAMPSIE HILLS
- MILNGAVIE
- GLASGOW

INTRODUCTION

I first walked the West Highland Way with Mike McQueen, a close friend and fellow photographer, in December 1990, some ten years after it had opened as a fully integrated route. A couple of months earlier, washed out of our tent during a climbing holiday, we took refuge in a hotel and found it full of walkers. It turned out that they were walking the West Highland Way, and, as we traced the route on someone's map, it looked interesting. Another day of rain found us scouring Fort William for material on the walk, but finding little. And so the idea for this book began to take shape.

In the year that followed I walked the West Highland Way four times, in December, March, June and September, and made many shorter trips along it - from a half-day stroll to three or four days' walking. Mike's record is much the same, and we know the route pretty well now. It is a walk of great charm through rich and varied scenery, of no difficulty if your feet are hardened to long-distance walking, and which needs no special skills such as climbing, or even map-reading. However, it's not a 'wilderness experience'. Apart from three sections: the last day on Loch Lomond-side, the crossing of Rannoch Moor, and from Kinlochleven to Glen Nevis, you are never far from busy public roads or railways; each night's stop is near a village or hotel, and most lunchtimes, if you want, can be spent in a pub. And yet all this 'civilisation' need never intrude. On the first morning, you walk off the platform at Milngavie station to plunge into Mugdock Woods (so it seems), and in a few moments have left the world behind. All along The Way, it takes only a screen of trees, a fold in the ground - or a certain attitude of mind - to shut out any reminders of what you have come here to escape.

From the oakwoods on the east side of Loch Lomond, dappled with sunlight and echoing to bird-song, you can look across a mile or so of calm water to cars and trucks scurrying up and down the A82, and laugh at your good fortune. But you can use that same road to leap-frog bits of the walk if you are short of time, or to escape altogether if the weather has become really hideous (something not totally unknown in the West Highlands!). It may be your wish to get away from people for a time by doing the walk, but the hotels, b&b's and bunk-houses offer the companionship of The Way. Of course, they also offer food, hot baths and comfortable beds, which many walkers may welcome at the end of another day of foot-slogging! The beauty of the West Highland Way is that you can shape it to suit your own needs: go in the most popular months of July and August, staying in hotels and b&b's, or go in December and camp along the way, and you will

Waymarker, Glen Nevis

have two very different experiences. Follow the route exactly as in the guides, or climb as many Monroes as you have time for; there are no rules. A survey carried out by the Forestry Commission, five years or so ago, indicated that around 70,000 people were walking The West Highland Way each year, in whole or in part, and numbers have probably increased since then. It is a tribute to the Ranger Service, and the Forestry Commission which looks after so much of the trail, that, in spite of these huge numbers the paths are excellent, and only rarely are there seriously wet or eroded stretches. There is a problem of litter, however. Even among walkers there still seems to be a minority who take a perverse pleasure in disrupting camp-sites, dropping litter and causing annoyance. This can only cause further difficulties, with farmers and estate owners becoming less amenable. There are already too many "Private - Keep Out" and similar signs scattered around the Scottish Highlands. The situation must be avoided where, in the face of large numbers of walkers - only a very few of whom cause nuisance or damage - landowners react with new restrictions or exclusions. The traditional freedom to roam the Scottish hills is increasingly precious in these high-stress times, but long-distance walking routes have a high profile, and to an extent may concentrate environmental damage. This is a long-term problem, and we should work towards improving the uneasy relationship between countryside users and owners; in the meantime, all walkers should act responsibly, and perhaps landowners could be a little less fearful of the hordes they imagine are going to descend on them from the cities, wreaking havoc.

As a city dweller all my adult life, any visit to the Scottish countryside is both a return to my roots, and a powerful charge to the spiritual batteries. To go again and again to the West Highland Way was to experience this differently, on each trip finding something new, and learning better to observe and record the landscape I love so much. In writing the short text which accompanies our pictures, I have tried to convey some of my excitement at just being there, and my enthusiasm for the Scottish Highlands and nature in general. It seems miraculous that in this mechanised age, and in spite of all the hazards of pollution, acid rain, habitat destruction and so on, we still have on our doorstep such a wonderful and inspiring resource.

After our initial failure to find any existing material about the walk, I soon discovered that there are two excellent guide-books still in print - Tom Hunter's original guide, and the HMSO official handbook, written by Robert Aitken. I am indebted to both, but have tried to avoid simply repeating what they do so well. Therefore I don't deal with the history, or the geology of the walk, or how to get from A to B, but with how it was 'on the day' - each episode being taken from diaries I kept of all my walks.

When we started out on this project, our aim was very much to walk the route as often as was needed for good photographic coverage. Over the year represented in the book, much changed, and simply doing the Way and really getting to know it, took over to the extent that photography almost became secondary. But not quite. Photographers are not like other people, and it's sad but true that for many of us, there's often no real enjoyment in being out in the countryside unless photography is also involved. This obsession (though it charitably could be described as professionalism!) led to constant pre-dawn starts (to get the best light); to the carrying of absurdly heavy packs full of gear and film, and to an exhausting search for ever better camera positions, sometimes far from the trail. Much of this might be regarded as masochism by other walkers, but I hope that some of our results in this book can be seen as justifying these apparent excesses. We decided, early on, to use only medium-large format camera equipment in order to obtain high-quality results. This had other consequences, including the absence of wild-life pictures from the book, since these large cameras were too slow and noisy for wild-life work. I did most of my walking in the winter and spring, since I love the light at that time of the year, and because the trail is quieter then. (For exactly opposite reasons I never ventured on The Way during July and August; also because these are the midge months in the Highlands.) This brought logistical problems, since some of the facilities along the Way are closed 'off-season', but compensated with some sought-after solitude, and the grandeur of the winter scenery. It may also explain the large number of mentions that bad weather gets in my diary! In photographing The West Highland Way, Mike and I were liberal in our definition of it. Therefore mountains alongside The Way could be climbed to get camera positions; rivers crossing it followed to interesting stretches, and items of note near, but not always visible from, The Way could be visited. Our subjects were the beauties of nature and the landscape. We had a great deal of enjoyment in taking these pictures, and in making all the walks that this entailed. It was often hard work but never less than fun, which is how it should be for everyone who walks The West Highland Way.

David Paterson, Clapham, London, June 1992.

Conic Hill and Loch Lomond

SOUTHERN APPROACHES

3 December, Milngavie to Drymen. 7.20 a.m. on a clear, frosty morning - we stumble from the Glasgow to Milngavie train, still bleary with sleep, and hoist packs for the start of our first walk up the West Highland Way. The transition from town to country is startling - under a bridge, down a short stretch of empty street, turn right - and in moments we are under the trees of Allander Park. On this crisp winter's morning, on the edge of what feels like an adventure, it seems hardly real that only minutes ago we were cursing British Rail for the lack of breakfast at Glasgow Central, still less that an hour ago we were dozing on the night-train from London. Now we are both in high spirits, and there is keen anticipation as well as frost in the air. Bare trees are outlined against a blue-black sky, and a full moon is setting as we quit the fringes of the town - the only other creatures moving are a man and his dog, taking a walk in the early-morning air. On the edge of the woods, pale rushes line the banks of the Allander Water and rustle in a breeze which comes up with daybreak. Panting up the first short slope, we look back at the town from a bare hillside above the trees, to watch windows light up as the houses of Milngavie come alive at this breakfast hour. Beyond, to the south, is the haze of Glasgow.

Mugdock Woods are still in darkness as we tramp along, making quick time on a good path, but the first signs of wild-life are appearing; a grey squirrel darts for safety, a pair of magpies rise from the undergrowth as we pass, and from the depths of the wood comes the call of a pheasant. Little else stirs, and there's no other sound except our boots as we crunch up the trail. Out of the woods, a pale sun veiled by thin cloud glints from the waters of Craigallian Loch, and a robin watches from the shelter of a bush, creeping further into shadow as I stop to look. Beyond the loch, the wide and well-made trail divides a conifer plantation fringed at its southern end by oaks, where drifts of brown leaves hint at winter, though the trees still cling to the last traces of their autumn colours. Across the Blanefield road a brief climb leads to open country with a promise of hills, and at the watershed Strath Blane lies below us. The distant bulk of Ben Lomond, streaked with last month's snow, dwarfs its nearest neighbours; and Conic Hill which we pass tomorrow, is tucked low on the horizon below the Arrochar peaks.

11 February, Dumgoyach. A hard east wind sweeps down over the rim of the Campsie Hills and a thin covering of snow is re-freezing and crackles under our feet. In the dying light of late afternoon, Dumgoyach Hill - a tree covered volcanic stump - looms above, rising abruptly from the floor of the valley, its steepness giving it a presence out of all proportion to its small size. The standing stones, in this light, are brooding and mysterious, and it's easy to understand why an ancient people might choose this place for their rituals. Their megalith stands in a shallow arc apparently pointed towards the hill, and the stones, shifting slowly through the ages, lean in the same direction, with the large centre-stone aimed straight at the summit. The wind is too bitter, and the light fading too quickly for much picture-taking. Fingers nipped, and toes beginning to ache with the cold, we scuttle back across the field to rejoin the trail.

3 June, Milngavie to Drymen. After several solo trips, Mike and I are together again this time, and we are away and walking by 6.30 a.m. to get the early light. In Mugdock Woods, the trees I could barely recognise in winter have been transformed by new leaves into a mix of elm, ash, sycamore, birch, rowan, hazel and, predominantly, oak, with a rich undergrowth and a canopy open enough to let the sunshine through. There is a chorus of birdsong, so different from the silent woods of winter, and where the trail approaches the Allander Water, a heron rises with its long, slow flap, to settle a few hundreds yards upstream. By the loch-side we lose the sun for a while as a skein of high cloud rapidly fills the sky, and rather than pass by too much country in flat light, we decide, in the interests of photography, to stop a while and see if the weather improves. In this brief rest, and as we dawdle along the trail between Mugdock Wood and Dumgoyach Hill, some twenty walkers pass, one lunatic carrying a ghetto-blaster with Radio One blaring. (Radio Three might have been preferable but even that would drown the natural sounds of the woods!) Last December, in a whole week, we saw just three other walkers, and I know which season I prefer.

Garadhban Forest

Near the hill a pair of plovers rise with their eerie cries to circle closely around us; they must have a nest near the trail and remain in great distress until we move on. Ahead, Strath Blane is a wide valley, dotted with stands of conifers, and with farms and houses in sheltered corners. Above, to the east, the ramparts of the Campsies bask in sunshine, but the wind is cold and far to the north the hills beyond Ben Lomond show signs of fresh snow. Whin, broom, buttercups, marsh marigolds and the buds of flag-iris make splashes of yellow all the way from

Milngavie to Dumgoyach, and blossoming trees of rowan and horse-chestnut stand like beacons in the landscape; hawthorns in full bloom gleam through the darker passages of the woods. White and grey clouds sail on an azure sky, and hot sun alternates with the north wind and squalls of icy rain. In the afternoon, clouds press in to cover the sky, and in a freshening wind we scurry up the track, past wild rose bushes where blue-tits forage cheerfully among last year's rose-hips. At Gartness, picturesque on its bend of the Endrick Water, a 'Private' sign graces every garden gate; the last two miles of tarmac road to Drymen seem endless, and there is more than a hint of soreness about the feet, at the end of a fourteen-mile day. In the town, the room above the pub is expensive and dreary, with cheap and broken fittings, a sagging ceiling and ill-fitting door; downstairs the jukebox goes till midnight. In the morning we are up early and away without breakfast.

Waymarker, Arlehaven

4 June, Conic Hill. Above Drymen, the entrance to Garadhban Forest is through acres of bright yellow gorse, and on the very fringe of the forest there is the sweet smell of hawthorn. Under the trees, the path is broad and bright, but darker patches of the wood close in from time to time. On an afternoon of quickly changing weather, the trees provide occasional and welcome shelter as icy showers come hissing into the canopy on the north wind, and in quieter moments pigeons coo, or occasionally crash out through the branches above our heads. After an hour or two of easy walking we emerge from the trees to space and sunshine, with Conic Hill just a mile away across an open moor. The haul up from the Burn of Mar, cascading through groves of silver birch, is straight into the wind and seems longer than a mile. This moorland and steep little hill is a foretaste of the Highlands to come, and Conic Hill lies virtually on the Highland Boundary Fault - a major geological feature where the older sandstones, granites and schists of the Highlands strain against the younger rocks of the Lowlands. The last few hundred feet up the hill have me sweating and slightly out of breath, but the climb is actually very short and we reach the top in minutes. On the summit, sharp squalls of sleet and hail sweep over as we cower beneath waterproofs, only to leap out, cameras ready, whenever the sun appears. Between showers, the rain-washed air is clear as crystal; to the south, the pastoral Lowland scenery lies green and open, and, far in the distance now, the tower-blocks of Glasgow gleam through a gap. Northwards the rough texture of the Highlands takes over, the landscape colours change from green to brown and the horizon is hemmed around by peaks. Below, Loch Lomond alternately glowers darkly and shimmers silkily around the line of islands, pointing west, which marks the Highland fault line. After two hours of watching and waiting for that special magic to happen - we don't know what - we give up the vigil. In the evening sun, yellow streamers of cloud drift across the southern sky, and flush slowly to pink. The wind gets up again and raises a brisk chop on the loch as we head off downhill through larch, spruce and good Scots pine, to the flesh-pots of Balmaha.

24 September, Balmaha. A lunch-stop in this now familiar village, where today a cold wind is sweeping in off the loch, and spray mixes with drops of a hard rain blown from clouds a mile or two to the west. Not knowing whether either of Balmaha's food-stops would be open, I am carrying something for lunch - the usual sort of delicacies - two squashed sandwiches bought yesterday, a bruised apple, and the wrapper from a bar of chocolate, eaten an hour ago in a fit of greed in the lee of Conic Hill. Not finding a really comfortable nook to shelter in, I brave the wind by sitting out at the end of the little pier, eating my cheese and pickles to the sound of waves smacking into the stanchions below. Soon cold, I pick up my pack and set off, chewing, for Rowardennan.

Between Balmaha and Rowardennan, the official trail meanders between the loch-shore and the motor-road, which it uses for quite long sections. I decide to stick strictly to the shore rather than the trail, in the hope that the extra walking will be rewarded by a more interesting afternoon. A long shingle beach just north of Balmaha has lines of dried leaves and pine-needles showing previous high-water marks, and good sized waves roll in over the stones. Beyond this beach a series of rocky headlands, with trees pressing close to the shore, makes for slightly harder walking, though here and there outcroppings of sandstone provide pavements as level as any city street. Further easy walking on open shores is interspersed with minor scrambles at rockier sections, until, somewhere beyond Sallochy I am forced up off the beach by steep cliffs descending straight into the loch. Above, I rejoin the trail through beautiful oakwoods whose canopy rustles in the breeze off the loch. The path, which cuts across behind Ross Point for a mile or so, turns away from the water. Emerging eventually from the trees, I find movements in the clouds giving hopeful signs that some sort of change in the weather may be on the way, and walk on northwards with one eye on the sky, where patches of blue are making slow but determined progress.

The entrance to Mugdock Woods

Frost-coated grasses, Allander Park

Overgrown tree root, Mugdock Woods

Early morning, near Dumgoyach Farm

Ferns, near Carbeth Loch

Craigallian Loch, Mugdock Country Park

Early mists, Carbeth Loch

25

Mossy stone, near Arlehaven

Campsie Hills from Arlehaven

Dumgoyach Standing Stones, Strathblane

Storm clouds over Campsies, from Conic Hill

Loch Lomond & Inchcailloch Island from Balmaha

Woods between Conic Hill and Balmaha

Balmaha Pier, Loch Lomond

Early mist over Loch Lomond, from Luss

A Walk on the Wild Side

A WALK ON THE WILD SIDE

5 December, Balmaha to Inversnaid. After a late start on a morning of wind and rain we hitch a lift from Balmaha to Rowardennan, where the locked and shuttered hotel puts paid to any ideas of whiling away a few more rainy hours in a warm, comfortable bar. At the rocky headland beyond the hotel, spray is falling into the trees near the water, and Loch Lomond is black and choppy. A little farther on, a head pokes out of a semi-collapsed tent where two Liverpudlian walkers have passed a not-too-comfortable night; they are damp, but cheerful. Round the corner, the youth hostel is also closed at this season and has a blank, deserted look. It's a relief to find the shelter of the trees, beyond the hostel, away from the penetrating wind. Across Loch Lomond, traffic on the A82 is constant - a stream of north and south-bound cars and trucks, tiny at this distance but whose noise is just occasionally brought to us on the wind. On this side of the loch, especially now that we have left behind all roads and habitation, there is a growing sense of remoteness which is very welcome. In this winter weather, with last night's stop seven miles behind, and tonight's maybe as much as fourteen ahead, we feel truly on the wild side of Loch Lomond.

Waymarker, Dubh Lochan

All around, the hills have their heads in cloud, and though the rain comes and goes, the threat is always there. Occasionally the wind will tear a rent in the clouds, and for an instant there is a gleam of blue; but it's fleeting, and the sun never shows. The walking is easy and pleasant, with deep piles of leaves under the trees and many of the more sheltered oaks still carrying some autumn colour. From the undergrowth of holly, birch and alder, comes the piping of small birds, and by the trail, two piles of feathers within five meters show where a predator has made recent kills. At a split in the trail we separate - to be able to photograph both routes - Mike taking the lochside path, while I get the easier forest road. The walking is uneventful, and I make few stops; treetops sway in the wind and raindrops spatter the trail around me; a lone sheep, strayed from somewhere, watches nervously as I pass. Where the two paths rejoin, guessing that Mike will have been slower, I wait a few minutes in a shower of rain until he appears. From the loch comes the slap of waves, and along the last miles to the hotel there is the constant sound and sight of streams, fed by the rain, rushing down steep slopes from Ben Lomond hidden in cloud above us. In a rising wind and heavier rain the hotel at Inversnaid finally comes in sight through the trees; improbably, it is open and has rooms available (we are not carrying tent or sleeping bags), which we happily take.

6 December, Inversnaid to Inverarnan. Eternally hopeful for that beautiful early morning light, we are away from Inversnaid just after eight into a still-dark morning which quickly turns to steady rain. The path, *good enough at first*, soon becomes a welter of slippery tree roots and boulders, and we stumble along, muttering and cursing the whole idea of walks, West Highland ones in particular. (This is one of those occasions when one's reasons for doing this kind of thing tend to get closely examined, and though I am strongly motivated to get into wild and remote places to take pictures - a desire frustrated in bad weather - I know that ultimately I deeply enjoy the physical challenge of climbing and walking, even in the worst of weather.) Rob Roy's Cave, greatly romanticised by Sir Walter Scott, is a dark gash below tumbled rocks, half-hidden in the undergrowth, and there's little else to take our attention, focused on the treacherous ground under our feet, until Doune Bothy hoves into view. The empty bothy is redolent of woodsmoke, soot, and our own warm damp clothing: a not unpleasant mixture, familiar but unexpected, an echo from the forgotten farm bothies of childhood, or the trail-side villages of Nepal where I have done most of my long-distance walking. Soon we have a fire crackling in the hearth and clothes steaming gently in the heat; after the restorative powers of a hot drink and some food, even the rain outside seems something only to laugh about. We allow ourselves a brief half-hour's rest, then douse the fire and go. Out of the bothy, another gap in the clouds opens to show blue sky, but is snapped shut in seconds, and at the Dubh Lochan we turn to look back down the slope towards Loch Lomond, nearly lost to sight in the mist and spume. At the lochan, a heavy squall of rain hisses in the reeds, streams rush in brown spate down the hillsides, and a bedraggled sheep watches from the shelter of a fallen tree. The Dubh Lochan marks the highest point of this section of trail, and once over the little col we run off downhill to the pub at Inverarnah, a couple of miles away, to dry out over a pint and some lunch. We don't rush this part; the afternoon's prospect is another long wet walk to Crianlarich.

7 May, Rowardennan. Just a short walk in the woods north of here today, up the loch-side by the shore path, and back by the forestry road. On a day of high cloud and pleasant southerly breezes, every bird in these oakwoods is singing, and the forest-floor is rich with the colours of spring flowers. The first rhododendron buds are reddening and, in every clearing, broom and whin are in full flower. But it's not Eden; by the loch-side a scatter of white and brown tufts of hair and a smear of blood on the rocks shows where a fox has made a meal. Across the loch, Ben Arthur flirts with cloud; overhead a soft shower of rain rustles in the leaves but gives way to sunshine, the first of the day. A herd of goats wanders across the track, adults watching me with calm, almond eyes, kids frisking among the rocks, and as I turn to go back down towards Rowardennan, the first of the morning's quota of north-bound walkers is puffing up the track. Hanging under a tree along the loch-side, a gaping boot dangles by its laces, with a message attached: 'This boot was made for walking,/ But it will walk no more,/ It packed in two miles down the track,/ And now my feet are sore.' At least he could still laugh.

10 May, The Dubh Lochan. A few hours of beautiful evening light - enough to walk from Inverarnan to the Dubh Lochan and back. There are sheep with young lambs in the fields now, and the trees are clouds of fresh green, from the barely-open buds of oak, to the mature leaves of sycamore beside Beinglas Farm. A mile beyond the farm, another of the herds of feral goats straddles the track; a pure white billy has a beard so long it touches the ground as he walks. Along the hill-side the late sun is still warm, but at the lochan a wind shivers the reeds around the fringe, and the sun hides in slow-moving cloud; fish are rising, and from the far shore a heron lifts away. Climbing the hill above the loch, views open out in every direction, though the sun has now dipped behind the western ridges, and only the top of Ben Lomond is still touched by its yellow light; Loch Lomond shines pale silver far down among shadows. On the summit of the hill, a tiny lamb lies dead; sheep graze unconcernedly all around, not much given to senti-mentality. On the way back to Inverarnan, slow-moving pools of the river Falloch reflect the evening sky turning red, and a dipper flits from rock to sand-bar in the gloaming. the last mile is walked beneath a glorious sky of deepening colour, with the first stars just showing.

25 September, Rowardennan. In this last week of September, the wind is incessant, and with it the rain that sweeps in from the Atlantic to Scotland's north and west. I had unavoidably missed a glorious spell of weather earlier in the month, and then waited impatiently as day after day the forecasts gave most of Britain blue skies and sun, but the Highlands wind and rain. With other commitments loom-ing, I had decided to take a chance with this particular week, and so far it has been exactly as the Met. Office predicted - dull, wet and windy - and on this third morning of the walk I have yet to take a photograph. A mile beyond Rowardennan, where the trail divides I take the easier, high level route along the forestry road. In these conditions I will have quite enough of the twists turns, tree roots and boulders of the loch-side path this afternoon, when there is no other way from Inversnaid to Inverarnan. In steady rain, I plod up the easy slope for a couple of miles, giving thanks for the shelter of the trees. Near the high point on the road the trees thin out, and on a good day there would be fine views across Loch Lomond to the Arrochar Hills; today the far shore is barely visible through

Doune Bothy

the mist and rain, and the occasional slight clearing of the atmosphere serves only to show that the cloud-line is just a couple of hundred feet above the water. It's very reminiscent of the first time I walked this section with Mike last December, except that it's not so cold, and trees are still in full leaf (I had been hoping to find some early autumn colours, but perhaps because of the long wet summer, everything is still very green).

At Inversnaid I deny myself the pleasure of getting warm and dry in the bar, because I would just have to come out and get wet again. Beyond the hotel, the well-made portion of the trail is all too quickly behind me, and for two hours I struggle through a morass of tangled roots and branches, slippery rocks and deep mud. I had often heard this stretch of trail described as 'difficult', and for the first time understand why, as I slip and slide along three miles of trail which, in the wet, have come to resemble an army obstacle course. At last, Doune Bothy appears through the trees, with a wisp of smoke at the chimney, and, cheered by the thought of human company and the chance of a shared moan at the weather, I speed up for the last few hundred yards. But the bothy is empty, with the last remnants of a fire dying in the grate.

There's no change in the weather before Inverarnan, and the hotel is full. The lobby is certainly full of rucksacks and muddy boots, and in the bar an obvious throng of walkers is deep into pints and tales of heroic disregard for anything Scottish weather can throw at them. It is hard not to join in, and for half-an-hour we polish our self-images as hard men of the hills, before it's time to catch the bus up to Crianlarich for bed and breakfast. (Or should I just roll up in my cagoule and sleep under a hedge, like a real hard man?). On the way to Crianlarich, a watery sun puts in an appearance and I cross my fingers for tomorrow.

Beech tree at Balmaha

Frosted ferns, south Loch Lomond-side

Loch Lomond at sunset

Camus an Losgann, Loch Lomond-side

North Loch Lomond and Arrochar Hills

Arrochymore Point, Loch Lomond

Evening at Sallochy, Loch Lomond

Stob nan Eigbrach and Loch Lomond

Inversnaid Falls

Early morning, Loch Lomond

Pollochro Nature Reserve, near Inversnaid

Loch Lomond-side, near Rowardennan

The Dubh Loch, above Ardleish.

Abandoned farm at Ardleish

The Ben Glas Burn, near Inverarnan

Trail through larch plantation, Crianlarich

6 December, Inveraran to Crianlarich. We delay as long as possible our departure from the pub after lunch. Once you are warm and dry, having been cold and wet, it's hard to go out and get wet all over again. The rain is so heavy that Mike and I opt to follow the main road, where the contrast with the morning's walk up the last stretch of Loch Lomond-side, empty of any other human presence, is complete. Heavy traffic swishes past in both directions, completely ignoring our presence, and though occasionally I stick out a thumb, there seems very little hope of any motorist stopping to let two wet, muddy backpackers into his nice, clean car. The Falls of Falloch are felt rather than seen, through a curtain of rain, mist and spray, as the water thunders through a neck of rock, and the flow is so great that there is barely any separation between the falls, the normally tranquil pool below them, and the rapids which flow from the pool. Today, there is just a great surge of brown water, vertical as it comes over the fall, then foaming out and down the rocky gorge with awesome power. Higher up Glen Falloch, the mist, which has

Waymarker, Tyndrum

come with the rain, clears to reveal a landscape of bare hills dotted with Scots pines, many of which are dead or dying. As in many northern glens, intensive grazing by sheep and cattle, and deer as well, prevents regrowth of native woodlands, and this 'savanna' looks to be in a state of terminal decline. Although, geologically speaking, the Way enters the Highlands at Balmaha on Loch Lomond-side, somehow it's here, where the thickly wooded and intimate scenes of lower Glen Falloch give way to the broad mountain landscapes in the upper part of the valley, that the Highlands really seem to take over. As we rejoin the trail to cross the main road above the farm at Derrydarroch, there is a feeling of crossing some sort of divide; we have left the Lowlands behind.

Beyond Derrydarroch, further rain comes sweeping down the valley, obscuring everything, and does not lift again before Crianlarich. Squelching down the last mile to the village, a question keeps recurring: is this really a viable project. or have I just come up with another hare-brained scheme which will keep me away from my family for frequent longish spells, while I struggle with mounting frustration and weeks of 'Scottish' weather (as my Japanese wife calls it, scornfully)? There's no honest answer to that.

7 December, Crianlarich to Bridge of Orchy. Heavy grey cloud is down on all the tops, but enough can be seen to know that the hills have a good covering of snow down to below 2,000 feet. Here in the valley the snow is falling thick and fast, and only a short distance out of the village we are plastered from head to foot. We agree, with very little argument, to cheat by taking the train to Tyndrum.

Streams are still swollen from the rain of the two preceding days, and rush down deep-cut gullies into the gorge of the Chrom Allt; near at hand, steep ridges are picked out by the new snow, and the landscape is a stark black-and-white. Below Beinn Dorain, invisible in the murk, a large herd of highland cattle stands around disconsolately, munching wisps of straw, while sheep huddle together in a hollow, backs to the wind. Higher on the hill, a small herd of deer graze, apparently oblivious to both the snow and our presence. As we get near Bridge of Orchy, the snow stops suddenly as if a switch had been thrown, and the wind begins to ease; the northern clouds lift ever so slowly and a patch of the palest blue appears. But it's a tease; within minutes all this is reversed, and it's snowing heavily again. At Bridge of Orchy station, in mid-afternoon, Mike jumps on a southbound train which happens along at precisely the right moment; he has camera problems, and hopes to get things sorted out in Glasgow. By bedtime he's back with a replacement, proving that British Rail does occasionally have its uses.

9 February, Crianlarich to Tyndrum. Almost four inches of soft new snow on the trail today, and not a human footprint to be seen once outside village. The air is cold and marvellously still; a few snowflakes drift down from high clouds thin enough to hint at sunshine later; trees hang heavy with snow; sounds are muffled; in the distance a truck grinds uphill. Along the trail there are many animal signs, and as well as sheep, there are footprints of deer, rabbit, hare and fox. Frequently, the beneath-the-snow runways of mice can also be seen, and the fox has followed the path for many hundreds of yards, since these mouse-tunnels show up most clearly against its even surface. Along a quarter-mile of trail the fox has pounced seven times on mouse-tunnels, and four times a tiny drop or two of blood gives silent witness to a kill. The sun never does get out: instead the clouds thicken and a wind gets up. By St Fillans Chapel it's blowing snow straight into my face, and before I reach the shelter of the trees near Tyndrum, the conditions are arctic.

29 March, Tyndrum. My main objective today has little to do with making progress along the walk, but instead is to climb the hill immediately north of

Tyndrum - Beinn Odhar - which will give good views north to Beinn Dorain, and the Way around its lower slopes. As ever, I want to be out at first light for the sake of photography, and, good at early rises when I need to be, I'm away from the hotel in semi-darkness before seven. By the time I reach the foot of the hill, about a mile out of the village, the first sun is just lighting the tops; down here, there's still blue shadow in the valley and thick rime on the grass as I move up open slopes, watched by a flock of recumbent sheep. At the shoulder of the hill, a frozen stream leads down from a large snow patch, and above, the upper slopes are crossed by a fence whose uprooted posts dangle from tight-stretched wires. Even higher on the hill, a twin-strand electric fence, about knee-high, its wires loose and tangled in the grass, runs right over the hilltop and down the southern ridge. Neither spectacle makes a very good advertisement for concerned estate management. At the summit, the views are superb, with Beinn Dorain to the north and Beinn a Chaisteill close by to the east; at a greater range there are snow-caps in every direction, a little lost in the haze. For a few minutes I luxuriate in that unique feeling which comes from being alone on a mountain-top.

Tucked under the northern slopes of the hill, two steep snow-fields are as hard as iron, and I retreat from the middle of one, stepping gingerly, aware that without axe and crampons, a slip could be embarrassing. As I reach the summit rocks again, a shadow sweeps silently over; a hundred feet above, an eagle drifts effortlessly over the void. For ten minutes or so I watch her quarter the ground south of the summit: in that time, she flaps her wings just once, then soars up and off to the north, and in moments is a speck which fades into the blue. On the descent towards the broad ridge of Meall Buidhe, there comes the repeated plaintive whistle of an unseen bird; in a flattening of the ridge a tiny lochan mirrors clouds and blue sky; below, in the gully of the Chrom Allt, pied wagtails bob and glide in their peculiar flight.

Coming into the village past the general store, around noon, I exchange greetings with my first human being of the day. After a solid pub lunch and a long rest, I set out southwards for Crianlarich in warm afternoon sun, through woods redolent of warm resin and ringing with birdsong.

8 June, Tyndrum. At this half-way point of the walk, I'm again taking an easy day out to have a rest, write up some notes, clean and sort out gear, and generally laze around a bit. In the afternoon, I set off to explore an area of Caledonian pine-forest a couple of miles to the south-west. The way out of the village follows a path south through pleasant mixed conifers bordering the Chrom Allt. After half-a-mile, the trees stop abruptly at a wide area of what looks like alluvial deposits, but is actually a relic of old lead-workings. Another half-mile beyond the trees, a curious circular pond lies in a hollow just off the trail, the distant Crianlarich hills reflected in its waxy surface, and round a corner the River Cononish tumbles through a series of rocky rapids and miniature falls. I follow the river west to pick up a good track heading for the pine woods. The trees, which from a distance appeared quite densely packed, turn out to be well-spaced and another example of what is now termed 'savanna woodland'; though this may just be another name for a dying natural forest. Certainly there is no sign of new growth anywhere, and though the trees are fine specimens, they are very old. Its a beautiful, timeless place, where it's easy to imagine yourself in the Scotland of centuries ago, before the great Caledonian forest was destroyed. The trees stand on a carpet of short grass, heather and pine needles; there is no animal life visible, only the tinkling of small,

Falls of Falloch

unseen birds and the picked-over bones of a Cheviot ram - large, judging by the size of the horns - which lie in a hollow below a group of particularly lovely pines. Another forty minutes of walking, uphill now in the heat of the afternoon sun, bring me to the upper limit of the forest, on the slopes of Beinn Dubhchraig. From a vantage-point above the trees, their canopies make a sea of dark green which rolls gently in the breeze.

Apart from the constant buzz of insects, there's no sound or movement, and the landscape has a timeless quality. Visually, it could easily be the time of Robert the Bruce, who fought a battle near here. After a defeat at the hands of the English, he was beaten by his enemies the MacDougals in a skirmish at Dalrigh ('The King's Field') near the chapel of St Fillans. He is supposed to have fled south after the battle, to go into hiding in what much later became known as Rob Roy's Cave; but what is more certain is that Robert the Bruce supported the monks of St Fillan and gave them his protection, a privilege maintained for them in later years by the Scottish Crown. In Bruce's day, most of the Highlands were still forest-covered, and the remaining pockets, like this one, are reminders of what has been lost.

On the stroll back down through the trees, a distant clatter announces the return of the twentieth century, and a Glasgow-bound train rattles its way slowly down the line.

River Falloch, lower Glen Falloch

Ferns, lower Glen Falloch

Autumn colours in Glen Falloch

Derrydarroch Farm, Glen Falloch

Hawthorn blossom near Keilator Farm, Glen Falloch

Stob Glas, upper Glen Falloch

Old BR rolling stock, Crianlarich Station

Beinn a Chroin, from the trail leaving Crianlarich

Lone tree, looking to Ben More above Crainlarich

Autumn leaves near St Fillans Chapel

From Tyndrum, looking south to Crianlarich hills

A82 from Beinn Odhar, outside Tyndrum

Sunrise at Bridge of Orchy

River Ba and The Blackmount, before sun-up

8 December Bridge of Orchy to Kingshouse. We had planned for an early start today, but the fierceness of the weather makes us wait at least until daylight. A thick covering of overnight snow and a hard north wind driving snow before it, makes the thought of the shelterless miles across Rannoch Moor distinctly unappealing. Finally, in a brief lifting of the weather at 9.10 a.m. we set off from the hotel at Bridge of Orchy. The wind never lets up and the cold is bitter, but the clouds part and for a time there is bright sunshine. New snow squeaks underfoot as we take the bridge over the partly frozen River Orchy; icicles hang in roadside ditches. Across the river, we soon gain the shelter of the trees for the short climb over the ridge, the Mam Carraigh, between the river and Loch Tulla, and for a time the sun almost feels warm, making us sweat inside winter clothing and windproofs. The track is criss-crossed by animal tracks, and half-way up the slope a pair of grouse rise clattering from under our feet, almost giving me heart-failure. Otherwise there is little sign of life. At the top we get the full force of the wind again, but the sun is shining on a glistening panorama. Looking back east over the treetops, the three biggest of the local peaks - Beinn a Chreachain, Beinn an Dothaidh and Beinn Dorain present a wall of gleaming snow which rarely falls below 3000 feet, and to the north-west the Rannoch hills have plumes of spindrift blowing from every top. Rannoch Moor itself is an undulating sea of white, where the only feature is the black circle of the yet un-frozen Loch Tulla.

The sunshine stays with us until the hotel at Inveroran, when clouds suddenly loom in from the north, and within moments heavy flakes of snow are whirling out of a darkening sky. For a couple of miles we have the partial shelter of young plantations on one side of the track, and are not totally exposed to the northerly gale, but eventually we run out of shelter and the wind takes us full in the face. Head down, we plod without a break as far as Ba Bridge which the guidebooks suggest can provide some shelter *'in extremis'*. You would certainly have to be desperate to stay under the bridge for longer than it takes to eat a bar of chocolate, which is what we do, while the wind eddies around us from all directions, blowing spindrift into every conceivable aperture. As soon as possible we head off again. In spite of the weather there is no danger or even real difficulty; we are both well clothed and equipped; (comparing notes later we found that we had both greatly enjoyed this experience of Rannoch in a blizzard), and the old Glencoe Road, which is followed across the edge of the moor, makes navigation straightforward. The only hazard is the occasional patch of old ice hidden under new snow; this can be very slippery indeed, and both of us take falls before it dawns that a little more caution is needed. At the little col below Beinn Chaorach, there is the briefest lull in the weather, the wind drops a notch, the snow stops and for a moment there is a gleam of sun. Back down the track, Craig an Fhirich appears as a blunt wedge wreathed in spindrift; no other hills are visible, and in seconds even this apparition is blotted out by a curtain of blown snow. The rest of the way to the Kingshouse is tramped in the teeth of the renewed blizzard. At the hotel we are pleased to find that our time for the thirteen miles into this wind, including stops for photography and 'lunch', has been a minute or two over five hours.

7 February, Forest Lodge. After a short mild spell which has removed most of the recent snow, low temperatures have returned and all surface water on Rannoch Moor is deeply frozen. As I walk on to the moor from the road-end at Forest Lodge there are brief flurries of snow, but these are soon replaced by mild sunshine which lasts throughout the day. At a corner of the track the local estate has put out bales of straw for the deer, but today these are ignored and half-a-mile away a large herd of hinds and last year's calves graze on a sunny knoll. Deciding that it is too far to reach and get back from Ba Bridge in daylight (this matters only for photography), I climb a small hill off to the left of the trail, for good views of Stob Ghabhar and the Clach Leathad. On the

Mam Carragh, Bridge of Orchy

walk back, two young stags have found the straw, and, intent on their meal, are unaware of my approach. When I am about fifteen yards away they suddenly realise something is up, and leap away in alarm. As is often the way with stags, their curiosity gets the better of them, and within a few yards they slow to a trot, then stop to look back to see who or what is this interloper. Lower down, in the first trees above this side of Loch Tulla, a buzzard lifts heavily away from a fencepost; in woods warmed by the low, yellow light of late afternoon, a roebuck crosses the trail a hundred yards ahead, also without seeing me - then suddenly does, and darts into the trees, leaping over mounds and tussocks of grass; at a safe distance he stops a moment to look back, then races off.

6 June, Beinn Toaig. Another day dawns with an unbroken blue sky; only the breeze, which has come all week from the north, keeps temperatures down a little and makes walking bearable. From a camp at the bridge behind Inveroran, I will take a morning out to climb Beinn Toaig, the southern spur of Stob a Choire Odhair, which is the hill immediately above Victoria Bridge. There may be new or unusual views of the route across Rannoch Moor from its summit, and anyway, it's a fine day for climbing. The climb is very easy and quite uneventful, but views over the moor are superb, and improve with every little gain in height. As usual with a long ridge like this, there are several false summits, and I'm just starting to feel a slight sense of annoyance at being fooled yet again by something as inanimate as a mountain, when at last a tall cairn comes into sight. Right by the highest rocks a ptarmigan suddenly appears at my feet, chirping pitifully and trailing both wings as if injured. Clearly, there is a nest very close by, and not wishing to step on eggs or chicks, I stay still a moment, studying the ground immediately ahead. This sends the bird into a frenzied pretence at injury, an Oscar-winning performance in which she comes near enough to brush my boot with her outstretched wing. As I take a step, nine or ten chicks burst out from behind a large rock and run off in all directions, squeaking madly. So that they won't run too far, and to allow the hen to gather them without too much difficulty, I stride off briskly. She follows closely by me for at least two hundred yards, then gradually falls behind as she realises that I really am going away. At last she turns and scuttles back up the hill to her chicks. Some moments later the cock bird swoops down over my head, to land a few hundred feet lower down in Coire Toaig. Taking the shortest route back to Forest Lodge, I start to descend in that direction, heading south-east from the summit, and am surprised to have to thread my way through a couple of lines of short crags. As I stand on the top of the last one, looking for a convenient way to climb down, a red-deer hind trots out from beneath me, closely followed by a fine calf, still in dappled coat; they stop to look up at me, then take off rapidly over the ridge to my right, and are gone in seconds. The rest of the descent is straightforward, and progressively hotter; in an hour I am back at the tent in the kind of sweat which only a plunge in a cold river will banish.

27 September, Rannoch Moor. Today another ambition for this particular walk will be abandoned. Because I am travelling more lightly than usual, I had planned an early start from Bridge of Orchy, to cross to the Kingshouse not by the track, but by a high-level route over the tops of the Blackmount. Yesterday's weather was an improvement on the preceding few days, and today's forecast was, at least, ambiguous enough to give rise to some hope, but when the alarm wakes me at

Rannoch Moor, looking south to Stob a Choire Odhar

Beinn Achaladair & Beinn an Dothaidh from Forest Lodge

Rannoch Moor trail below Druim a Bhlair

Loch Ba and the Clach Leathad, Rannoch Moor

Ba Bridge, Rannoch Moor

Rannoch Moor from the summit of Meall a Bhuiridh

Buachaille Etive Moor, from the Glencoe ski-slopes

Craig an Fhirich in spindrift, Rannoch Moor

Buachaille Etive Beg from near Altnafeadh

Climbers on Buachaille Etive Mor

Lagangarbh Cottage, Glencoe

Autumn trees in Glencoe

Buachaille Etive Mor and the River Etive

Glencoe from above Altnafeadh

Buachaille Etive Mor from the Kings House road

Carn Dearg and shoulder of Ben Nevis from Glen Nevis

9 December, Altnafeadh to Kinlochleven. It's a gloomy morning, as we set out at about 9 a.m. Heavy cloud is down on all the tops, and there are rain-drops on the wind. We go easily up the winding track of the Devil's Staircase, to the high-point at 1,800 feet. Some lightening of the sky and a hint of blue tempts us to stop for photography, but as so often on these occasions it's a false promise, and soon the clouds have closed in again. The north side of the ridge has been denuded of snow by the wind, and streams are mute, frozen solid; the path is a sheet of ice, unbroken for hundreds of yards at a time. Setting foot on it can have only one result, and you count yourself lucky if you fall on a lump of heather rather than rock. In the distance, the Mamore Hills are dappled with sunshine, but the air is thick with haze and for the most part the landscape lies like lead under a sullen sky. Coming down into Coire Mhorair we move suddenly from winter back into autumn; birches and alders still have a trace of leaf, there is grass and bracken underfoot, and green moss lines the banks of burbling streams. Following the huge pipelines which bring water down from the reservoir to power the aluminium plant, we stroll into Kinlochleven on a shaft of afternoon sunlight.

10 December, Kinlochleven to Fort William. This is the last day of our first walk along the West Highland Way, and there's no doubting that we feel a sense of achievement. The sun is shining from a calm blue sky on as fine a December day as you could wish for, mist spills down the hillside from the Blackwater Reservoir and the frost is sharp as we set off along the old military road up the Lairig Mor. There is ice on the track here, too, and small streams are silenced by the frost; larger streams rush noisily among icy boulders, and in the upper glen, mist lies densely where the sun has not yet reached. On a day too fine to stay earth-bound down here in the valley, we turn uphill by the ruins of Tigh na Sleubhaich for the col west of Stob Ban on the Mamore Ridge. For the lack of any obvious path up the coire, we just forge straight up the centre, and in no time we are above the snow-line. Sheltered from the breeze and fully exposed to the now warm sun, we are soon toiling under our heavy packs, and good humour is temporarily lost.

On reaching the ridge the agony is proved worthwhile as the landscape opens in front of us, and southwards rank upon rank of peaks - Glencoe, Glen Etive, Blackmount and Cruachan - crowd in on each other until they are lost in haze. To the north, Ben Nevis raises its great rounded hump out of a sea of mist that stretches from beneath our feet to the horizon; east and west along our ridge, the

Mamores are etched against the blue. Rock-hard drifts of old snow lie under the ridge and in every gully; otherwise the summits have been scoured bare by recent winds, and the merest skim of new snow doesn't cover the ground but is just enough subtly to alter all the colours. Sneaking along the ridge below the main summit of Stob Ban, we cross a couple of minor tops and descend the long ridge which the mountain throws down into Glen Nevis. The last miles down the glen are under the same thick blanket of mist that lay below us only an hour ago and everything in the valley is thickly coated with rime; nothing stirs on this most windless day of the entire walk; sounds are deadened. We walk another hour along the road in silence, each lost in his own thoughts; at the Youth Hostel we guzzle cans of fizzy drinks, and, deciding that honour has been satisfied, declare this to be the end of the walk. Summoning a taxi, we ride in comfort to Fort William, and take a bus to Glasgow.

10 February, The Mamore Ridge. A late-ish start on a day of ringing blue skies and bright sun, with very little breeze. Mike sets off to walk the official route to Fort William, while I climb again to the Mamore ridge. After a couple of days of illness caused by food poisoning, I am feeling quite fit again, and set off due north from Mamore Lodge into Coire na Ba, following the left bank of the stream on a trail curving around the base of the ridge which falls from Sgurr a Mhaim. Climbing up the west wall of the coire in glorious sunshine, I soon discover my error, ending up on a narrow platform with cliffs above and below, and no viable onward route. To retrace my steps and descend to the coire floor is the only possibility, after which I re-ascend via a broad snowy ridge which leads to a subsidiary summit on the main ridge. Stunning views open

Waymarker, Glen Nevis

on every side as I gain height, and Ben Nevis and the peaks beyond glow in the afternoon sun. Under total snow-cover and an immense sky of deepening blue the hills assume Himalayan proportions; Am Bodach and Sgurr a Mhaim loom above me to the west, and to the east a shining ridge curves and dips before rising to the summit rocks of Na Gruagaichean and Binnein Mor. As a raft of broken cloud begins to fill the sky I descend to the col below Am Bodach, and traverse below the main peak and two minor ones, looking for a way back on to the ridge below Sgurr a Mhaim. But huge snow cornices overhang the whole length of the ridge, and, suddenly too tired to retrace my steps yet again, I turn and descend reluctantly into Coire a Mhail. Unless you climb out over one the surrounding ridges, the only way out of this coire is to descend the cliffs at its mouth where the Steall waterfall leaps four hundred feet into Glen Nevis. Below, I see that another lone climber, with whom I had chatted earlier in the day, has already gone down into the coire. I rush to catch up with him and hear with relief that he is fairly sure there is a safe route down into Glen Nevis. We agree to join forces for the descent of the cliffs to the west of the falls. Threading crags by connecting ledges, and more than once forced to re-ascend to find a continuation, we finally hit upon a series of snow-filled rakes and gullies descending at a steep but manageable angle to the valley floor. He goes down first, slashing steps with his axe in the hard and excellent snow; I follow, grateful for this help and with a rush of adrenalin banishing tiredness for a time. The long walk down Glen Nevis again becomes something of a trudge, brightened by the sunset painting the summits of the hills a vivid scarlet.

Bothy above Kinlochleven

25 March, Fort William to Kinlochleven. Fortified by coffee and bacon rolls in the station buffet, I'm away by 8.30 a.m., at the start of a north-south walk. It's another day of bright sun and blue sky, and in the bottom reaches of Glen Nevis, the river flows sweet and clear between lines of trees not yet showing any leaf, though catkins are in flower. The trail climbs steeply away from the glen through a series of firebreaks in the forest which covers the southern slopes, and here a sour note is struck on an otherwise perfect morning as on each side of the path, beneath every third or fourth tree, there is a pile of tissue paper (even soiled paper can be put in a plastic bag - along with cans, sweet wrappings and crisp bags - and disposed of properly later). As the trail flows on, eventually the garbage peters out; some wet sections are followed by a good forestry road, and a wooden staircase leads to a fine path through plantations of young spruce. Above the trees, Ben Nevis is snow-capped. Over the col below Sgor Chalum (the northern end of the Mamore Ridge) the sun is hot, and openings through the trees give fine views down towards the farm at Blarmachfoldach, and to where Loch Lunn da Bhra lies glittering in the sun. Round another corner, the long glen of the Lairig Mor stretches far ahead, empty, and when I am a mile down it, two Tornados come through at zero altitude like a clap of thunder; the noise rolls and echoes around the hills long after they have passed. Later, at the deserted farmsteads there's a silence made all the more oppressive by a loose sheet of corrugated-iron creaking in the freshening southerly breeze; far off, an unseen buzzard mews. The miles down to Kinlochleven are just a stroll on a fine clear afternoon turning into a cool evening, and later, after dark, I come out to star-gaze for a while on a night of crystal air and sharp frost.

11 June, Loch Lunn Da Bhra. A lunch-stop here on the last stage of what has been a wonderful early summer walk, with fine weather nearly all the way from Milngavie. Making early starts has given me empty trails most mornings, and time to rest in the middle of the day, when it's too hot for comfortable walking, and the sun is too high overhead for good photography. As is usual with me, my feet started to ache around the sixth day of the walk, and since then I have been hobbling a little. Or perhaps more than a little, since an hour ago I was caught up by a younger, fitter walker who turned out to have a chemist's shop of 'foot comfort' products in his pack, which he was quick to offer me. I accepted without hesitation, and in return shared a precious bar of Cadbury's Fruit and Nut - more than a fair swop, really. Now it's time to move on again; it's still hot, and the long climb up to the ridge, before dropping down into Glen Nevis, is punishing; but the deep shade of the trees is cool like water; downhill goes easy.

30 October, Glen Nevis. A fine autumn day of sun, breezes and showers, and I've stolen an hour or two from other work to try to photograph the autumn colours. Somehow, I'm not finding pleasing images, and for once I am content just to stroll and observe. There have been other days like this, when I could happily have abandoned cameras in order to walk, climb and enjoy; cameras can impose a burden, and get between you and the experience. But the task of photographing The West Highland Way has given focus to an entire year, and now that it's nearly over, I already have a sense of loss.

Cloud-shadows move across brown and russet hills; the River Nevis glides silkily between turf banks; dark conifers sway against the blue. These are the healing images we return with to our homes, in our memories as well as (better than) on film. Here, in this lovely glen, it's hard to grasp the reality of the threats facing our environment, and easy to dismiss problems as over-stated. I worry for the future of this walk, and all our countryside, though for now I am happy to have made my own discovery of the West Highland Way. I'll repeat the walk in the future, and I hope that many thousands of others will, too. It will still be here, if we play our cards right.

Iced-up boulder on Devil's Staircase

Stob na Doire and the Lairig Gartain, Glencoe

Kinlochleven and Mamore Lodge

Allt Coire Mhorair near Kinlochleven

113

Lairig Mor valley, above Kinlochleven

Ruin at Tigh na Sleubhaich, Lairig Mor

Loch Lunn Da Bhra and Meall a Chaorainn

Loch Lunn Da Bhra, frozen in mid-winter

Winter sunset, Loch Lunn Da Bhra

Grey Mare's Tail, Kinlochleven

Spruce plantation, Glen Nevis

Coire a Mhail, Mamore Hills

Sgurr a Mhaim, Mamore Hills

The Glen Nevis road in autumn

Walker on the Stob Ban ridge above Glen Nevis

Ben Nevis, from above Blarmfoldach

BIBLIOGRAPHY

GUIDES:
Tom Hunter 'A Guide to the West Highland Way', Constable, 1979.
Robert Aitken 'The West Highland Way' HMSO, 1980.
Information leaflet: 'West Highland Way - Long Distance Route', Countryside Commission for Scotland.
Map: The West Highland Way, Footprint Publications, Stirling. (Based on OS material, reprinted 1989.)

GENERAL READING:
F. Fraser Darling & J.M.Boyd 'The Highlands and Islands', Collins, 1964
J.B. Whitlow 'Geology and Scenery in Scotland', Penguin, 1977.
W.H.Murray 'Scotland's Mountains', Scottish Mountaineering Trust, 1987.
D.J.Bennet 'The Southern Highlands', S. M. Trust, 1972.
P.H. Hodgkiss 'The Central Highlands' S. M. Trust, 1976.
D. Nethersole-Thompson 'Highlands Birds', HIDB, 1974.
D. Stephen 'Highland Animals', HIDB, 1974.
D. Ratcliffe 'Highland Flora', HIBD, 1976.

PHOTO CREDITS

MIKE MCQUEEN:
Page nos: Front Cover, 1, 3, 10, 18, 20, 21, 22, 25, 27, 28, 32, 33, 34, 38, 42, 43, 44, 46, 48, 49, 50, 53, 58, 60, 64, 74, 75, 76, 79, 87, 90, 91, 94, 98, 99, 102, 103, 111, 114, 115, 116, 119, 124.

DAVID PATERSON:
Page nos: 5, 6, 9, 12, 19, 24, 26, 29, 30, 36, 40, 41, 47, 52, 54, 56, 57, 62, 66, 67, 69, 70, 72, 73, 80, 82, 84, 86, 88, 89, 92, 95, 96, 97, 104, 106, 108, 110, 112, 113, 118, 120, 121, 123, 125, 126, Back Cover.

ACKNOWLEDGEMENTS

All walkers on the West Highland Way are of course indebted to those who established it, not without some difficulty, and to the organisations and public bodies who pay for and maintain the route, namely, The Countryside Commission for Scotland, The Forestry Commission, the ranger service, and local government in Strathclyde, Central and Highland Regions. The landowners whose property is crossed are also due continuing thanks. My own gratitude is due to Iain Roy for his helpful comments on the text; to my collaborator Mike McQueen for some irreplaceable photographs and a consistently unselfish attitude during the picture-editing; to our designer Jonathan Allen for producing a great show-case for our work, and to Neville Moir and Canongate Press for sticking with us when others might not have; and last but not least to my family for putting up (again) with my frequent absences.

D. Paterson